FOLLOWING PRINCE CASPIAN

Further Encounters with the Lion of Narnia

THOMAS WILLIAMS

THOMAS NELSON
Since 1798

NASHVILLE DALLAS MEXICO CITY RIO DE JANEIRO BEIJING

© 2008 by Thomas M. Williams

Published in Nashville, Tennessee, by Thomas Nelson. Thomas Nelson is a registered trademark of Thomas Nelson, Inc.

Thomas Nelson, Inc., titles may be purchased in bulk for educational, business, fund-raising, or sales promotional use. For information, please e-mail SpecialMarkets@ThomasNelson.com.

Scripture quotations are taken from *Holy Bible*, New Living Translation. © 1996. Used by permission of Tyndale House Publishers, Inc., Wheaton, Illinois 60189. All rights reserved.

Library of Congress Cataloging-in-Publication Data available upon request.

ISBN 978-0-8499-1997-8

Printed in the United States of America
08 09 10 11 12 QW 9 8 7 6 5 4 3 2 1

CONTENTS

Chapter One

PRINCE CASPIAN'S NARNIA

HUNDREDS OF YEARS HAVE PASSED IN Narnia since the days of *The Lion, the Witch and the Wardrobe*. Foreign invaders from the country of Telmar have taken over the land, ridding it of talking animals, centaurs, fauns, giants, and other nonhuman citizens that formerly filled the mountains and forests.

A new way of looking at the world prevails in Narnia. The Telmarines hate wild, natural things, so they are destroying forests and ruining rivers to build their civilization. They have ushered in a new, "enlightened"

1

age freed of ancient myths and magic. It's a time of no-nonsense, practical thinking. The Telmarines have zero tolerance for belief in the old magical stories of talking animals, especially the accounts of a Lion called Aslan, Son of the Emperor-over-Sea who created Narnia. Though the old stories are forbidden, a few Narnians remain who have not forgotten them.

The king of the new Narnia is the Telmarine Miraz. He is not the rightful king; he seized the throne after murdering his brother—the true king and Caspian's father—when the prince was an infant. Caspian's mother died soon afterward, and the boy has been raised by a nurse whom he loves dearly. He treasures the time when she tucks him in at night and tells him stories of Old Narnia, when animals talked, fauns danced in the woods, dwarfs mined glittering stones and metals from the hearts of the mountains, beautiful dryads danced in the forests, and the great Lion Aslan often appeared.

But when Caspian innocently asks his uncle about the old stories, Miraz angrily tells him that none of them are true and that he must never think about them again. The king banishes the nurse and hires a tutor to train Caspian in the practical things he must know to be king of Narnia.

SHUNNING THE OLD STORIES

It's not too hard to see the resemblance between Caspian's Narnia and our world today. A new way of thinking is sweeping our schools, universities, governments, and media. Technology and materialism dominate today's worldview, and the old stories of creation, miracles, and a God who came down and died for us seem out of place. A growing number of people consider religion a superstitious fantasy, neither true nor relevant to real life.

As in the new Narnia, many expressions of belief are forbidden in certain venues today. Public prayer is forbidden in public schools, and even speaking of God is forbidden in many. Sharing one's faith is forbidden in many workplaces. Political candidates are ridiculed for believing in a creator. Christian organizations are banned from many college campuses. Christianity is on the defensive. To take it seriously as a foundation for a credible worldview or adopt it as a way of life is becoming an embarrassment almost everywhere except inside the walls of churches.

Don't you sometimes feel the effect of this thinking? How do you react to words such as *sinner* or *salvation*, to terms like *Bible believer, faith in God, the power of prayer,* or *absolute truth*? Do you feel uncomfortable, maybe reluctant to take these terms seriously because they seem so quaint and out of place? Maybe the term *absolute truth* makes you uncomfortable because you doubt whether there is such a thing or, if there is, whether it can be known. If you are a Christian, do you feel embarrassed to express your beliefs outside church settings?

If you experience any of these feelings even to a small degree, as most of us do at times nowadays, it's a sign that we're living in a time like Caspian's Narnia. The old beliefs that once defined our culture are being discouraged or even repressed. The intuitive understanding of basic right and wrong is fast disappearing. We live in an age that largely rejects the old explanations of why we were placed on this planet. The idea that we can have a relationship with a higher power who created us for a glorious destiny is slipping away. Instead, human beings are assumed to have no higher purpose than following our own desires and scratching our own itches.

A NEW WAY OF THINKING

The culture today tells us that the old truths were never really true. What's true for you may not be true for me, so you and I must find our own truth. Absolute right and wrong are considered repressive, outdated concepts; after all, what's right for one person may be wrong for another. Therefore, the argument goes, others have no right to impose on you their idea of what's right and true. You must decide such things for yourself.

You may be caught up in this way of thinking. Maybe you are now following your own "truth." Maybe you've bought into today's mantra that life is meant for pleasure, and you've filled your life to the brim with continual stimulation—iPods, online games, movies, concerts, cuisine, TV, drugs, alcohol, sexual encounters—so that there's scarcely a free moment when your senses are not bombarded with pleasurable sensations.

Maybe you've bought into the cultural idea that happiness is found in having it all. You work yourself to exhaustion day and night to fill your life with things—a newer car, a more upscale home, clothing to match your peers, up-to-date electronic devices, golf clubs, ski equipment, snowmobiles, motorbikes, boats. . .

Maybe you've bought into the idea of finding significance in your career, and you are doing whatever it takes to scramble up the corporate ladder, to build a successful business, or to get to the top of your field so you'll be admired and respected.

These are the values that have largely replaced the values of the old stories. Yes, our culture is strikingly like that of Narnia in Prince Caspian's day. The old truths are out of favor, discouraged, and sometimes even forbidden. The new order of the day is to live by the rules of a pleasure-saturated, materialistic, self-pleasing culture according to whatever standards seem to work for you. As we will see in the next chapter, this approach didn't work very well in Narnia, and I'm afraid it won't work very well for us today.

Chapter Two

CASPIAN FLEES
FOR HIS LIFE

SINCE NARNIA'S KING MIRAZ HAS NO son of his own, he is content to groom his nephew Caspian as his heir. As the boy grows, Miraz has him trained in sword fighting, archery, hunting, history, law, rhetoric, and other arts all kings should master. Unknown to Miraz, the tutor he hires to teach the prince academic subjects is a firm believer in the old stories. He secretly expands Caspian's knowledge of Aslan and the ways of Old Narnia.

But one night, the tutor awakens Caspian

and urges him to flee for his life. The queen has just borne a son, and the tutor knows the treacherous king will now kill Caspian in order to clear his son's path to the throne. The young prince escapes, riding south into the night toward the great woods on the border of Archenland.

THE KILLER CULTURE

Like Caspian, many people come to realize that their everyday environment is not favorable to their best interests. You may be one of these people. You may have reached the point where endless pleasure has become an endless bore. All you get from continually stimulating your senses are senses that want continual stimulation. The music must get louder; the movies, bolder; the video games, more intense; the drugs, stronger; the sex, kinkier. There's no end to it; the more you scratch, the more you itch. Nothing is ultimately satisfying, so you continually seek greater thrills. Pleasure is a merry-go-round spinning at an ever-increasing rate until all you can do is hang on or be thrown off.

You may have discovered that having more things doesn't cut it either. That new car you were so proud of quickly lost its luster and now seems ho-hum. The upscale house was great for a while. You reveled in the extra space and the oohs and aahs of friends when you gave them the show-off tour. But now the newness has worn off; a kitchen tile has broken, a spill has stained the carpet, and the commode has overflowed. It's just another average house. In fact, you wish you'd bought one like the Johnsons, who make no more money than you yet just built a home half again as large in a much better neighborhood.

Or perhaps you finally achieved the status you craved. After years of fighting tooth and nail, working hours of overtime, taking endless business trips, and attending uncountable client dinners, you got your corner office with "VP" following your name on the plaque. You can now gaze out at the poor drones in that maze of cubicles and know that every one of them envies you as you once envied your boss.

But how long did it take you to realize that the rat race didn't end with your promotion? It merely cranked up the pace, and you must now pedal twice as fast. Even worse, you just learned that your rival—who once worked in the cubicle next to yours—has been promoted to *executive* vice president, and your new status suddenly seems meaningless.

Worse yet, pursuing these goals may have saddled you with debt that keeps you awake at night. Stress may be killing you. Your schedule may be isolating you from your spouse and children. Your relationships may be shallow, short-lived, deteriorating, or broken. You may have succumbed to an addiction—to drugs, alcohol, porn, or Internet gaming. You may even have resorted to dishonesty or theft.

Or perhaps you haven't achieved your dreams, yet the struggle itself has brought its own set of griefs. In a world where you make your own truth and the culture defines success by pleasure, things, and status, disillusionment and the feeling of being on the outside looking in kill the happiness of many.

LOOKING FOR SOMETHING MORE

If your life resembles any part of what's described above, you may have reached the point where you realize that there has to be something more. The values of the culture are not working, and you desperately need to escape before they kill you. Even if you don't keel over with a heart attack, a stroke, or an overdose, the continued pursuit of these deadly goals can work at your soul like a nerve-killing toxin. It can deaden the part of you that longs to find real truth. Like Prince Caspian, you need to ride out as fast as you can if you expect to save your life.

But ride out to where? Caspian's tutor has told him that there is something more than what he has experienced in Miraz's palace, and the prince hopes to find the truth of the old stories. You may have been told that the old stories of Christ offer the truth, yet you are reluctant to consider them. Somehow they just don't fit with your world. They have the feel of fantasy. God coming to earth as Jesus, dying, rising again, heaven, hell, miracles, the badness of sin—these things just don't mesh well with today's world of high-speed, high-tech affluence. You fear isolation or ridicule if you try to explore the old stories.

But what if those stories are true? What if they could save your life? Maybe it's time to ride away from the killer culture as Caspian did and check them out.

Chapter Three

COULD THE OLD STORIES BE TRUE?

PRINCE CASPIAN FLEES SOUTH TOWARD Archenland, where his tutor has assured him he will be welcomed and sheltered. As he reaches the great forest bordering that kingdom, a fierce storm arises. Lightning flashes, thunder booms, trees crash and Caspian's horse bolts into the wooded darkness. A low branch knocks the prince from his saddle, and he lies on the ground unconscious.

Caspian awakens in the company of two dwarfs and a talking badger. They are discussing what to do with him. One dwarf says they will either have to kill him or keep him prisoner for life, for they cannot let him go back and betray their whereabouts.

"I say," interrupts Caspian, "you haven't yet found whether I want to go back. I don't. I want to stay with you—if you'll let me. I've been looking for people like you all my life."[1]

When the dwarfs and badger discover who Caspian is, they introduce him to many other talking animals, as well as centaurs, fauns, and a giant, all of whom acknowledge Caspian as their legitimate king. The prince is delighted to find that the stories of Old Narnia are really true.

OUR NARROW PERSPECTIVE

The Telmarine society in which Caspian was raised regarded the old stories as ignorant fantasies that only stupid and gullible people would believe. But when Caspian discovers the truth of these stories, he realizes that it's the world he fled that's abnormal and out of step.

We all tend to be heavily influenced by our own culture. We can hardly help it; our perspective is formed by what's around us—the way people live and think, their values, their outlook, their beliefs, their pursuits and goals. We did not experience the cultures that preceded ours, so our own culture becomes the norm to us. It seems right because it's all we've known.

Unless we make the effort to find out what was believed in the past and why, we're likely to accept contemporary values without questioning whether they are true and right or merely passing fancies of the moment. We're likely to be guilty of what Narnia's creator, C. S. Lewis, called "chronological snobbery"—passing sentence on previous beliefs as inferior on the assumption that the present is always an improvement over the past.

Every age tends to think that history always progresses, that today's knowledge and wisdom must be superior to that of yesterday. But you don't have to look far to see the fallacy of this assumption. The pyramids, Greek and Roman art and architecture, European cathedrals, Incan culture, Moses, Aristotle, Plato, Aquinas, Michelangelo, Leonardo, Shakespeare, Newton, Mozart, and hundreds of others attest to great wisdom and achievement of the past. It's simply a mistake to think that past ages were ignorant, superstitious, and unreasoning. Our present age may have superior technology, but it doesn't have a monopoly on clear thinking.

UPSIDE DOWN REALITY

When we look at the history of our nation and our world, we find that belief in God or some supernatural deity has always been the norm. We also find a common standard of behavior throughout our world. The basic principles of right and wrong have been the same since the beginning of history. Every society has had laws against murder, theft, and lying, as well as rules governing relationships, property, marriage, and sexuality. These laws have varied somewhat from one culture to the next, and there have always been violators. Yet a common core of morality has always been the norm, and all societies have looked to a supernatural deity as the judge of their behavior.

As we can see, it's our present age that is out of step. Not to believe in God, to push him to the sidelines and close him up in churches, or to deny his authority in our morals and relationships are radical departures from the way the world has always thought and believed.

To claim that there is no single truth, no

absolute standard of right and wrong, is completely out of step with history. To believe that everyone can decide for himself or herself what's right is not the norm. Our present culture is turning reality upside down. Our age has lost its solid footing on truth in pursuit of the glitter of materialism and pleasure, and in the process we've swept aside the timeless standards that stood in our way. We're like adolescents gorging on junk food while our souls starve, lacking the nutrients needed for life and growth.

INVESTIGATE THE OPTION

If the overwhelming consensus of history is that there are real values and a deity to whom we owe allegiance, shouldn't we pay attention? Just because our age has chosen its own path is hardly a good reason to discard the map. Most people who have thoroughly investigated the truth of Christianity have come away convinced that the past ages got it right. They have good reason to believe that God does exist, Christ did really die for us, and we can reestablish a relationship with a loving God who will lead us to joy.

C. S. Lewis himself was very much a product of his age—a brilliant Oxford scholar steeped in the atheistic philosophies of his time. Though an unbeliever, he was an honest searcher, so he objectively considered the old stories. Reason and evidence convinced him that there really is a God who created the universe, came to earth, died for mankind's sins, and rose again with the promise that we can follow him into an eternity of pure joy. Just as his character Caspian escaped the Telmarines, Lewis abandoned his atheism, endured the scorn of his academic peers, and became a thoroughly dedicated Christian.

If you have hit the wall of meaning-lessness after buying into the values of the culture, I encourage you to check out the old stories for yourself. They're not really old, you know. They are timeless—just as valid and applicable today as when they were first written down. The bibliography at the end of this book lists a few highly readable books that may help you in your search.

LEARNING
TO BELIEVE

AFTER PRINCE CASPIAN FALLS UNCON-
scious in the forest, his horse wanders back
to its stable at King Miraz's castle. Now Miraz
knows his nephew has escaped. His spies
discover that the prince has taken up with
the creatures of the old stories, so the king
assembles his army and pursues. Caspian
and his supporters retreat to Aslan's How, a
temple-like mound built over the great stone
table on which Aslan was sacrificed centuries
before. Besieged and greatly outnumbered,
Caspian blows the ancient Horn of Queen

Susan, a magical relic that summons help when Narnia is in trouble.

With the blast of the Horn, the four Pevensie children whom we met in *The Lion, the Witch and the Wardrobe*—Peter, Susan, Edmund, and Lucy—are instantly pulled from England to Narnia. While about a thousand years have passed in Narnia since their last visit, only one year has passed in their British world.

The children arrive at the ancient ruins of their own castle, Cair Paravel, where they meet the dwarf Trumpkin, whom Caspian sent to bring them to Aslan's How. Peter and his siblings choose to take a shortcut they remember from the past, but they find the landscape so changed and overgrown that they lose their way. After hours of detouring and backtracking, they grow tired and hungry. Tempers flare as they all push their own ideas about which way they should go.

At night they camp, and after all are asleep, Lucy hears Aslan calling from the darkness. He tells her to awaken the others; they must follow him. The others, however, cannot see Aslan, and they are reluctant to follow. Though it distresses Lucy to leave them, she is determined to follow the Lion alone if necessary. Edmund follows her, thinking she really may have seen the Lion, and the others grudgingly do likewise.

Aslan leads them down a hidden ledge in a river gorge and up the other side to Prince Caspian camp. As they follow, all of them begin to see the Lion—even the dwarf Trumpkin, who hadn't believed he even existed.

WHY DOESN'T
GOD REVEAL HIMSELF?

If Lucy could see Aslan, why couldn't the others see him? If God is really there and wants us to believe in him, why doesn't he make his presence more apparent? In *Prince Caspian*, Aslan no longer shows himself in Narnia because people no longer believe. The culture itself has rejected him.

Lucy sees Aslan because she has been the most receptive to his ways and the most sensitive to his creation. She senses his presence in the stars and trees, and has been the least argumentative and most understanding of the children.

You see, God is a "gentleman." He doesn't intrude where he's not wanted. He made you free either to choose him or reject him, and he will not violate that freedom by forcing himself on you. If he overtly revealed himself to you, the option to believe would be removed. You would be forced to believe. God wants you to *want* to see him.

How can you want to see God? Essentially, by desiring what he offers. Or even by feeling a need for what he offers. If you've found that the values of the culture leave you empty, you've reached a good starting place: you feel a need. God offers meaning and joy through a relationship with him, but you have to want meaning and joy enough to follow him as Lucy did. Keep pursuing your own way, and you will continually backtrack and take detours. You'll never find what you're looking for.

THE KEY TO BELIEF

"But," you may ask, "isn't that putting the cart before the horse? How can I commit to following God before I even know he's real? If I've spent a lifetime pursuing the values of the culture, surrounded by friends, family, and peers all doing the same thing, how can you expect me just to suddenly believe in a dying and miraculously risen

God who can remove my guilt, love me dearly, and offer me an eternity of love? Why should I risk turning my back on what I know and plunge into a seemingly fantastic unknown?"

Well, for one thing, what have you got to lose? If you've found that pleasure, ambition, and wealth don't cut it, why stay in that rut? Staying can only hurt you. Caspian might never have left his Telmarine life had he not found out that he would be in mortal danger if he stayed. He plunged into the unknown in order to save his own life; he stepped out not knowing where his journey would lead him. If you know that remaining where you are will wither your life into a dry shell, why not risk a new path that promises something far better?

The fact that you can't know before you plunge must not deter you or you will never get out of your current trap. An unborn baby cannot know that coming into the world will give her a life of greater opportunity and more potential for joy than she can find in the safe comfort of the womb. Likewise, a caterpillar might choose never to become a butterfly, preferring its known world of abundant chewable leaves. But until it gives up that world, it can never soar.

I'm not recommending a blind plunge into the dark. Blind faith is not wise; faith should always be based on reasonable evidence. You should definitely investigate the truth of Christianity before you take the plunge. Read the New Testament. Listen to the experiences of people who have tried the new life it describes. Look at the lives of real Christians—not nominal Christians who talk the talk but don't walk the walk—and see the joy and love in their lives. Ultimately, however, you can never know that a new experience is truly good until you take the risk of trying it. Yes, you should look before you leap, but you still have to leap.

One of the strongest influences on C. S. Lewis was the nineteenth-century Scottish writer George MacDonald. MacDonald's story "The Golden Key" features two children, a boy named Mossy and a girl named Tangle, on a quest to find "the land from which the shadows fall." On their perilous adventure, they become separated from each other, and Tangle, now alone, loses her way. No one can help her until she meets the Old Man of the Fire:

> Then the Old Man of the Fire stooped over the floor of the cave, raised a huge stone from it, and left it leaning. It disclosed a great hole that went plumb-down.
>
> "That is the way," he said.
>
> "But there are no stairs."

"You must throw yourself in. There is no other way."[2]

That is exactly what it's like to follow God. You must take the plunge if you want to learn the truth. You must approach God not as a medicinal or a mechanical solution to your problems, but as a wild adventure into joy. You find the truth not by explanation, but by living. You get just enough direction and evidence to assure you that a good outcome is likely, and then you must take a deep breath and throw yourself in. There is no other way.

In *Prince Caspian*, Lucy took that plunge when she saw Aslan; she followed courageously even when she was not sure the others would. But perhaps even more courageous was her brother Edmund, who could not see Aslan but followed anyway because he trusted what Lucy saw. And the farther he followed, the more clearly he began to see something real leading him forward. First, Edmund saw just a shadow, an occasional glimpse of something he thought was there. Then, as he went on, the shadow solidified, and Edmund saw Aslan himself leading him toward his goal.

The same can happen to you.

Chapter Five

THE COMPANY OF BELIEVERS

ONE OF THE BIGGEST REASONS PEOPLE don't follow God is that doing so often means turning away from their family or peers. This was Lucy's dilemma. Even though she could see Aslan and the others couldn't, she could hardly stand the thought of leaving her companions and following the Lion into the wilderness alone.

It's surprising how hostile family and friends can be to the idea of following God. For whatever reasons, those entrenched in the values of the culture often seem to do all they can to make it hard on the person who wants to try the way of Christ.

I think this hostility stems mostly from a sense buried deep inside that by following Christ, you are doing the right thing. They, however, lack the courage to leave what they've been raised to believe. Your choice seems to judge them and put them in the wrong even though that is not your intention.

They judge themselves because the real truth has been implanted deep in everyone's heart. It's part of our original standard equipment. Everyone has within an innate sense that there is a supreme being and a true standard of right. We must be conditioned or educated into disbelief. Most often, disbelief is simply absorbed from those around us—family, schoolteachers and classmates, friends, coworkers. . . It's hard to take God seriously when those you're close to don't. It's not easy to go it alone. But if you find the path you're looking for, it's worth all the rejection or ridicule you might feel.

The good news, however, is that you don't have to go it alone. Affirmation, help, companionship, and support for your decision are readily available.

THE COMPANY OF THE OLD STORIES

Immediately after leaving Miraz's castle, Prince Caspian feels courageous and excited about his new life. But the feeling doesn't last. Soon he encounters rain. The landscape is unfamiliar, his path is unknown, and the world he faces seems strange and daunting. To make matters worse, he is alone, and he begins to feel terrified and small.

After his runaway horse abandons him in the forest, the creatures of the old stories rescue Caspian, take him in, welcome him, nurture him, and—with the exception of one distrustful dwarf—consider him part of their company. His fear and loneliness vanish. He finds his rightful place among the new company and soon feels very much a part of them.

Caspian quickly discovers that the company has a common goal. The old Narnians seek a better way of life than the usurping Telmarines offer. Now, with the legitimate Narnian king among them, they prepare to take back Narnia, restore belief in Aslan, and bring joy back to the land. Feeling a powerful loyalty to one another, they give strength, support, and encouragement wherever and whenever needed. This common goal strengthens Caspian's bond with his newfound family and gives him meaning and purpose.

THE COMPANY OF BELIEVERS

A company similar to Caspian's is available to you today. You can join people who believe in the old stories about a loving God who created men and women to know joy. You can adopt their mission, which is to know God better, grow closer to him, and participate in restoring a society that is turning away from him and headed for disaster. You can join a company that upholds solid, absolute, dependable truth and strives to live in conformity to that truth.

You can find these companions in your neighborhood church. The church is a band of believers encouraging one another to follow God and stand strong in the face of adversity. The path is not lonely or difficult when you are in a company of believers who love, support, and encourage one another with fierce loyalty.

THE IMPERFECT COMPANY

You may have been tracking with me until I urged you to join a church. You may not be too keen on churches. Maybe you've had a bad experience with a church. Maybe you've heard throughout your life that all church members are hypocrites. Maybe you've seen church members engaged in questionable business dealings or outright immorality. Even if you haven't seen this personally, you've certainly seen it in the news. *So, you may wonder, why should I join a church? I can be just as good a Christian without it.*

Well, first of all, you can't. Just as a soldier will not survive a battle without the support of other soldiers, you will not survive as a Christian without the support of other Christians. Christianity means relationship. Christians thrive on relationship. Our relationship with fellow Christians is a primary way of experiencing our relationship to God. The apostle John wrote, "If someone says, 'I love God,' but hates a Christian brother or sister, that person is a liar; for if we don't love people we can see, how can we love God, whom we cannot see?"[3] A great joy of Christianity is being part of a people attempting to treat one another with the same kind of love and respect that they would give God if he were among them. Love binds the company together.

Second, it's a mistake to keep aloof from a church just because its members are imperfect. It's a widely held misunderstanding that Christians are always better than other people. The fact is, all Christians are imperfect works in progress. Christians have human weaknesses like everyone else.

Churches are not showcases that display polished Christian machines. They are more like repair shops where broken machines get fixed up and restored. Churches that function as they should are somewhat like support groups for addicted people: we are all "sin-aholics." We are all addicted to sin in general, and each of us is addicted to some specific sin that we find almost impossible to resist. The difference between Christians and non-Christians is that Christians recognize their sin addiction and take steps to deal with it. So the church is a company of fellow sin addicts bonded together to support one another and lead one another to place their lives in the hands of a higher power.

Similarly, Prince Caspian's company was far from perfect. They were sometimes discouraged, they bickered, they disagreed on strategy, and they occasionally irritated one another. But isn't that how it is in any family? And isn't it a good thing when people love one another enough that they accept each person's imperfections and yet keep on caring? We can find that kind of community in a good church just as Caspian found it in Old Narnia.

Chapter Six

JOY IN NARNIA

IF OUR FOCUS ON THE CONFLICT between Christian values and culture has led you to believe that Christianity is all difficulty and opposition, it's time to flip the coin. *Prince Caspian* explodes that notion like no other Narnia story does. In spite of the fact that Caspian had to fight against unbelievers who opposed the old and true ways of Narnia, he found his new companions to be a society characterized by great joy, laughter, dancing, and feasting.

The wildest celebration in all the Narnia books occurs in *Prince Caspian* when the creatures gather around Aslan before their march against the Telmarines. The tree spirits, birch-girls, willow-women, queenly beeches, and shaggy oak-men begin to dance around the Lion. Soon others enter the dance, including a youth wearing a fawn-skin (who turns out to be Bacchus, the wine-god) with a swarm of wild girls. The dance accelerates to a frenzy. Vines sprout and run everywhere, throwing about grapes that taste sweet beyond imagination. The air rings with laughter and shouting and yodeling. Aslan stands in the midst of it all, thoroughly approving.

THE SLANDER AGAINST CHRISTIANITY

Christianity often bears the stigma of being against anything fun—drinking, dancing, partying, hearty eating, and sex. This accusation is outright slander. Nothing could be further from the truth. Christ attended so many feasts that his enemies accused him of being a wino and a glutton. He often sparked up his parables with humorous exaggeration, as in the story of a man removing a sawdust speck from another's eye while a log hangs from his own. Jesus even made a hundred gallons of wine for a wedding party. He was no lofty, out-of-touch, head-in-the-clouds, fun-hating stick-in-the-mud. The Narnian celebration is an accurate picture of Christian joy.

God made us for joy. He created a world of incredible beauty, tastes, sights, sounds, and sensations, and he gave us five senses to take it all in. He created us to delight in all creation.

Yes, there are rules. Why? Because God knows us. We have trouble controlling our appetites. We will grab too much of a good thing and hurt or kill ourselves with it. So God gave us rules to regulate how we approach the good he gives us. The rules tell us how much, when, how, and with whom we can taste the delights of creation. The rules are not there to dampen our enjoyment, but to enhance it—to show us how to get the most joy without hurting ourselves (or anyone else) in the process. We have rules not because our desires are wrong, but because they are strong. The steed is meant to be ridden, but it is spirited and powerful. We must know how to use the reins.

All pleasures are meant for our delight, but no pleasure is safe without Christ. The principles of Christianity remove the danger and enhance the joy. As Susan said to Lucy after the wild dance in the forest, "I wouldn't have felt safe with Bacchus and all his wild girls if we'd met them without Aslan."

"I should think not," Lucy replied.[4]

FINDING REAL JOY

Am I saying that if you become a Christian, suddenly your life will be a continual feast, a dance, a party? That all difficulties will disappear, all relationships will be ideal, and nothing but good times will fill your life? No, of course not. No one can avoid pain. Disease, accidents, grief, and tragedy are part of the condition of this messed up world—for the Christian as well as the unbeliever.

The idea is not that Christians can be joyful because they have no troubles; they can be joyful in spite of the troubles they have. For people without hope, this life is all there is, and any kind of trouble is like a rainstorm ruining their picnic. Christians, on the other hand, can plow through their problems and pains with great equilibrium because they know that nothing can destroy their tomorrow. And because their tomorrow is secure, so is their today.

One of the great writers of the New Testament, the apostle Paul, faced unthinkable difficulties. He was beaten, stoned, threatened, imprisoned often, and even ship-wrecked. Yet he was about the most joyful person you'll ever hear of. One night in prison after enduring a brutal flogging, he and his companion couldn't help but burst into song.[5] Despite the very real hardships he suffered, Paul often expressed irrepressible joy, and he urged all Christians to do the same.[6]

And why not? As a Christian, it's easy to be joyful. You have found true meaning in life. You have purpose and security because God loves you dearly, and nothing that happens can take that love away from you. Nothing. That is an enormous cause for joy.

Happiness, as our culture defines it, is an

emotion of the moment. It's always dependent on some pleasurable happening—a winning lottery ticket, a promotion, a day at the beach, a good steak dinner, a fun date. This kind of happiness is good, but it's shallow and fragile. Maintaining it depends on a steady stream of good luck, and any trouble can snatch it away. But the joy of belonging to God does not depend on good things happening. Christian joy is a solid, permanent, secure foundation underlying all of life. It endures even through the worst of trouble. And you can have it if you follow God as Lucy followed Aslan.

In *Prince Caspian*, Aslan leads a march toward the camp of the Telmarines. Joyful followers gather around him. As they come to Beruna, dancing with great merriment and joy, only a few townspeople catch the spirit and join the divine revelers. Most hunker down and remain stuck in their stunted, mundane existence. Why do people reject joy? Most simply cannot understand what it's really like because they have never experienced it, and there is no way to experience joy until you join the dance. You cannot know joy until you take that leap we discussed in the previous chapter and plunge into God's hands like a child jumping into a swimming pool.

Chapter Seven

BRINGING ASLAN BACK

As Prince Caspian opens, the Lion Aslan has not been seen in Narnia for many centuries. The reason for his withdrawal, as I have explained, is that the Narnians lost their belief in him. When his people no longer desire him, he leaves them to themselves.

And of course it was when Narnia was left to itself that things began to go wrong. The Telmarines conquered the country, and the land lost its magic. Narnia became a mundane, dull, practical land of selfish, greedy, joyless people.

Aslan did not return to Narnia until people began to believe again. More specifically, he did not return until believing people began to act on their belief. It's one thing to say, "I believe," but the words mean nothing until people are willing to back up their belief with their behavior. Sure, you can say you're a Christian because you believe the right truths, but belief without action is like a lightbulb without electricity. It's meaningless, and it makes no difference.

Prince Caspian acted on his belief. When he left the world that raised him and entered the world of the old stories, he rallied the believing creatures, and they began to make serious plans to take back Narnia for Aslan. When opposition hit in the form of the Telmarine army, Caspian blew the ancient Horn of Queen Susan—a call for Aslan's help—and help came, partly in the form of the Pevensie children. But, more important, Aslan returned to Narnia and began to act on his people's behalf.

TURNING THINGS AROUND

Maybe you feel that God has abandoned us. You see a nation sinking under the weight of rampant crime, growing fat and indolent on wealth, torn apart by political strife, jaded by continuous sensual entertainment, and indulging in rampant immorality. At the same time, churches seem ineffective, unbelief seems to be growing, and God seems to have disappeared.

Or maybe you are among those who have been caught up in the values of the culture and have never had much use for God. You pursued wealth, pleasure, or ambition until you found them to be soap bubbles that popped in your grasp. Then you began to think, *There's got to be something more*. But you don't know where to turn to find that elusive satisfaction, security, meaning, and deep love that each of us desires with a longing stronger than anything else in our soul.

If either of the above paragraphs describes you, the answer is the same: call on God. Prince Caspian blew Queen Susan's Horn, an action that symbolizes prayer, and Aslan came. If you call on God as Caspian called on Aslan, God will come. If enough people recognize the bankruptcy of our culture, acknowledge its failure to bring meaning to desperate people, and call on God, this action will turn our nation around. God will return and give us the power to change our culture; he will bring the "magic" back to our land in the form of believers committed to truth and filled with love and joy.

But even if that doesn't happen—even if enough people do not call on God to turn our nation around—your calling on him will bring him into your life and turn you around. You will be able to find that company of believers just as Caspian found fellowship with the creatures of the old stories, and through their love, support, and encouragement, you will draw strength to live your life with meaning and deep joy.

NOTES

1. C.S. Lewis, *Prince Caspian* (New York: The Macmillan Company, 1951), page 55.
2. George MacDonald, "The Golden Key," in *The Gifts of the child Christ*, Vol. 1, ed. Glenn Edward Sadler (Grand Rapids: William B. Eerdmans, 1973), page 171.
3. 1 John 4:20.
4. Lewis, *Prince Caspian*, page 133.
5. Acts 16:22-25.
6. Philippians 4:4.

BIBLIOGRAPHY

The following popular books present the case for belief in Christianity from several viewpoints.

Mere Christianity by C. S. Lewis
   Probably the most influential book on Christianity written in the twentieth century. An insightful guide to Christian belief, rationale, and behavior.

The Problem of Pain by C. S. Lewis
   A carefully reasoned answer to the unbeliever's primary objection to the existence of a powerful and loving God.

More Than a Carpenter by Josh McDowell
   Historical, logical, documentary, and scientific evidence verifying biblical accounts of Jesus Christ.

BIBLIOGRAPHY

The New Evidence That Demands a Verdict by Josh McDowell

A large reference book containing a wide range of evidence for the validity of the Bible, Christ, and the doctrines of Christianity.

The Case for Faith by Lee Strobel

A journalist investigates the toughest objections to Christianity.

ABOUT THE AUTHOR

THOMAS WILLIAMS's thirteen books include works of fiction, theology, drama, and three books on C. S. Lewis's Narnia. He has written one national best-seller and the Gold Medallion Award finalist *In Search of Certainty*, coauthored with Josh McDowell. A career designer-illustrator and C. S. Lewis aficionado, Tom's painting of Lewis hangs in the Wade Collection of Lewis manuscripts and memorabilia at Wheaton College. Tom and his wife, Faye, have three married daughters and eight grandchildren. They live in Granbury, Texas.

KNOWING ASLAN

AN ENCOUNTER WITH THE LION OF NARNIA

THOMAS WILLIAMS

THE PERFECT EVANGELISM TOOL FOR CHRISTIANS WHO WANT TO SHARE CHRIST WITH THEIR FRIENDS AND NEIGHBORS.

In addition to being one of the best loved books of all time, the movie *The Lion, the Witch and the Wardrobe* set box office records when it released Christmas 2005. Distributed by Disney, with special effects by WETA Workshop (*The Lord of the Rings*), and backed by a $150MM budget, *The Lion the Witch and the Wardrobe* drew millions of viewers, both Christian and non-Christian.

In the same way that Christians walk away from viewing Mel Gibson's *The Passion of the Christ* with a hunger to share Christ with their neighbors, Christians leave *The Lion, the Witch and the Wardrobe* wanting to share the Christ depicted by Aslan in the movie. Aslan, killed by the White Witch and raised to life three days later, is a shadow of the One who was crucified and raised to life for our sins.

Using biblical parallels, this small, easy-to-read book will lead readers to an understanding of Christ and what He did for them by drawing lessons from The C.S. Lewis book and movie. Christians will want to buy this book in bulk as a non-threatening, warm-hearted evangelistic tool.